Time to Refresh

A 21-Day Devotional to Renew Your .... ,
Sidelined

By Karen Brown Tyson

TABLE OF CONTENTS

INTRODUCTION

We all have busy lives. As women, we are wives, mothers, executives, entrepreneurs, athletes, teachers, students and so much more. Our days and nights are full.

We move from one task to the next. Picking up this and dropping off that. Sometimes we go on retreats, take vacations or carve out time for a sabbatical. We are always on the go.

But what happens when some part of our life comes to a screeching halt? Like when we get laid off from our jobs, or we don't get the job we want? We don't make the team, or something interrupts our education? What happens when we have one less thing to do on our to-do list? What are we supposed to do with our time while we sit on the sidelines of life?

I faced this question in 2017 when I got laid off. In my 25-year career as a professional communicator, this was my third time being laid off. My first experience was awful; I was a newlywed, and I wanted to do my part in contributing to our household expenses. But instead of being a happy, newly married woman, I was stressed, depressed, worried, angry, scared, and just plain miserable all the time. I was so anxious and desperate to get a new job I ended up taking a job at a public relations firm that was not a good fit. That was the year I learned about God's perfect and permissive will.

The second time I got laid off, I decided not to make the same mistakes I made following my first layoff. I vowed to walk in faith and not in fear, with a renewed mind. I spent three peaceful months taking care of my husband, our home, and working on ministry assignments at my church. I honestly believed God would lead me to my next exciting job, and He did.

On November 1, 2017, God blew the whistle a third time. After 16 years of devoted service, I learned that my company was making changes and that the team no longer needed me. Just like that, they cut me from the team. Rather than dwell in anger and unbelief, I thanked God and my boss for my time on the job, cleaned out my locker and walked out with a smile on my face and a grateful heart. I left, determined to make this layoff experience the best one yet.

When God calls timeout, we must listen

The word 'timeout' means a brief suspension of activity. In sports, a timeout allows for brief interruptions throughout the game where players can rest, talk about strategy with coaches or make substitutions. Just like an athlete, I used my timeout from work to my advantage.

Within minutes of hearing my job would be gone by the end of the year, I went to God in prayer. I asked God to speak to my mind. Out of my prayer time with God came a plan. A simple vision which focused on three key points:

> 1. Submission. I accept that God is in control of everything, including my layoff;
>
> 2. Faith. No matter what, I will walk in faith; and
>
> 3. Mind. I will resist all attempts by Satan to control my thoughts with negative thinking.

But I knew my little vision needed substance, so I asked God, "What do you want me to do during my timeout?" God, who knows me so well, gave me His answer day by day. Each day I focused on a different topic to study and key takeaways of what I learned. This book highlights the topics and takeaways God revealed in the first 21 days of my journey.

How to read this book

If you are a woman and God has ever called a timeout in your life, or if you have been sidelined, rejected, or told, "not this time," this book is for you. These next pages will guide you through 21 days of study where you will see how God moved in the lives of His people in the Bible.

Each day offers a glimpse into:

— the notes I wrote to myself over the course of 21 days

— a topic God asked me to focus on each day

— an example from the Bible that helped me see each topic in action

— my personal takeaways from each lesson

— advice on how to deal with real life concerns

To help you apply the lessons to your life, I offer my GLOW method, which stands for:

- **Grateful**-Each day we will end our lesson by letting God know how grateful we are for all He is doing during our timeout period.
- **Listening**-We will listen to God as we meditate and pray.
- **Observation**-We will pay careful attention to what God wants to show us in His Word.

- **Witness** - We will witness to others as we share our 'timeout' testimonies.

Open your heart to what God wants you to get out of this study. Ask the Lord to break through barriers and transform your mind as you study each topic.

My prayer is that you will gain a deeper understanding of God's plan for your life. I hope that you will come away understanding that when God calls a timeout, there's an opportunity to go through a transformation that will not only bless you but will deepen your walk with Christ.

Peace and blessings,

Karen

Note to Self:

Today I will do something I rarely do. I will clear my calendar. I am not taking any calls or going to any meetings or solving anyone's problems. Not today.

As I'm sure you know, God, I got laid off yesterday. After my boss and his boss told me everything they had to say, they said they understood if I needed time to process the news. So, I am taking time away today. Not because I am sad or depressed. I'm taking time to talk to you, Lord.

I'm excited! I can't wait to find out what you have planned for me next. I am using today to rest and abide in you, Father.

Speak to my heart.

DAY 1 - TIME TO REST

"Are you tired? Worn out? Burned out on religion? Come to me. Get away with me, and you'll recover your life. I'll show you how to take a real rest. Walk with me and work with me—watch how I do it. Learn the unforced rhythms of grace. I won't lay anything heavy or ill-fitting on you. Keep company with me, and you'll learn to live freely and lightly."

Matthew 11:28–30

During times of uncertainty, the enemy wants us fearful and anxious. But not God, who clarifies that we shouldn't worry about anything, but in

7

everything by prayer and supplication with thanksgiving let your requests be made known to God (Philippians 4:6). I found comfort in this Scripture when uncertainty came knocking on my door on November 1, 2017, with the news that my job was being eliminated.

I turned to Psalm 23 which outlines God's providential care. "The LORD is my shepherd; I shall not want," (v 1). From the beginning of this psalm, the reader can find comfort in knowing they have a loving and caring Savior, Jesus Christ, who will provide. Here are three things I took away from this Scripture.

Timeout Takeaways

Rest is part of God's plan

Because we all live busy, sometimes hectic lives, Christ must make us rest. The job of the shepherd is to make sheep take a break. And not just anywhere. Sheep are to rest in green pastures, suggesting a satisfying place.

God wants to restore my soul

In verse 3, David describes how his soul is restored by the tender care of the shepherd. Restoration is not about feeling better. In Hebrew, the words "restore my soul," mean "to bring to repentance." To honestly have our souls restored by God, we must repent.

Pursued by goodness and mercy

David describes how God blessed him in the presence of danger (v 5). Because God showed him such love and care, he was confident that the rest of his life would include goodness and mercy. We can count on God to do the same for us too.

GRATEFUL

What are you grateful for today?

LISTENING

As you pray, ask God to provide clear instructions on how and when you need to rest.

OBSERVATION

Read Psalm 23.

WITNESS

Talk to someone about how God takes care of you.

DAY 2—TIME TO PRAY

Note to Self:

It's 4 a.m., and I am wide awake. I am so grateful, Lord, for all you have done and continue to do. I had a great day yesterday. No emails. No telephone calls. Just peace and quiet.

I am so glad I started my job search already. I saw a few jobs I thought were interesting. I don't know where I will end up, but I do know this: I absolutely, positively DO NOT want to work anywhere you don't want me to work, Lord. I know that sounds crazy, but I've been there and done that. It was awful.

This time, I will pray for my next opportunity. Let your will be done on earth as it is in heaven. Grateful and excited about the day ahead.

Patiently waiting.

DAY 2 — TIME TO PRAY

"But you, when you pray, go into your room, and when you have shut your door, pray to your Father who is in the secret place; and your Father who sees in secret will reward you openly." (Matthew 6:6)

When Jesus said, "Go into your room," He wasn't trying to punish us. Instead, He is encouraging us to find a quiet place where we can talk to

God. Why? Because a life of prayer is not optional, it's necessary. Today, I will look at 2 Kings.

Prayer allows us to share our most intimate thoughts and feelings with God. In 2 Kings 20, King Hezekiah has just learned from the prophet Isaiah that he will die. After hearing this news, Hezekiah, "turned his face to the wall, and prayed unto the Lord. Please, Lord, remember me." (2 Kings 20:2–3). After hearing Hezekiah's prayer and seeing his tears, God not only promised to heal Hezekiah in three days, but he added 15 extra years to Hezekiah's life (v 6).

Timeout Takeaways

Prayer changes things

Whether there is a need for healing (2 Kings 20:2–3) or the request for blessings and an enlarged territory (1 Chronicles 4:10) going to God in prayer brings focus and change. Through prayer, not only do we get God's attention, but we also receive strength and power.

Understand prayer

At first glance, King Hezekiah's prayer, "Lord, remember me?" seems odd. It was as if he expected God to bless him based on his past behavior. But under the Old Covenant, blessing and cursing were based on obedience or disobedience (see Leviticus 26 and Deuteronomy 28). Therefore, King Hezekiah's prayer was appropriate. But it would not be suitable for present-day Christians. Under the New Covenant, we pray in the name of Jesus (John 16:23-24) on the principle of faith (Galatians 3:13-14).

God wants to hear from us all the time

God doesn't expect us only to pray when we are in trouble or sick. He expects us to pray regularly like David who prayed in the morning (Psalm 5:3) and Daniel who prayed three times each day (Daniel 6:10). Anna, in Luke 2:37, served God with fasting and prayer daily.

GRATEFUL

What are you grateful for today? `

LISTENING

As you pray, ask God to provide clear direction about what He wants you to understand about a life of prayer.

OBSERVATION

Read 2 Kings 20:2–3.

WITNESS

Talk to someone about how prayer helps during the tough times in your life.

DAY 3–TIME FOR FAITH

Note to Self:

Thank you, God, for waking me up this morning. It will be a great day!

When I logged onto my computer, I had a bunch of messages from coworkers offering support. Although, some messages were like condolences, "I'm so sorry to hear about the death of your job." Um, me too. :-)

Well, I can tell you I don't plan to lose faith. God, I believe you are in control. My prayer today is that you give me the words to say to those around me about my layoff. Let me show faith in a way that strengthens others.

Faithfully yours,

DAY 3 — TIME FOR FAITH

"And without faith, it is impossible to please him, for whoever would draw near to God must believe that he exists and that he rewards those who seek him." (Hebrews 11:6)

Scripture lets us know that without faith, it is impossible to please God. If we plan to have an ongoing, loving relationship with God, then faith is non-negotiable. In Mark 4:35–41, I found a beautiful lesson on faith.

Jesus and His disciples are in a storm. Fearful of the wind and rain, the disciples wake Jesus from a sound sleep (v 38). After Jesus calms the storm, "Then He said to them, 'Why are you fearful? Do you still have no faith?'" (v 40)

Sometimes we are guilty of acting like the disciples in the boat — afraid of everything. But God does not want His people to live in fear. When we remember how Jesus spoke to the storm saying, "Be still!" we can be confident that He can also speak to our storms. Here's what this Scripture taught me about fear.

Timeout Takeaways

Jesus is disturbed by unbelief

The storm did not bother Jesus since he was sound asleep. What disturbed Jesus was the disciples' unbelief after all they had seen Him do. Their disbelief meant they did not believe His Word.

God has not given us a spirit of fear

Understandably, fear is a natural feeling when faced with uncertainty. Don't have a job right now? Run to fear. Not asked to lead the PTA this year? Run to fear. Unable to afford your college courses right now. Run to fear. We've all been there. But we cannot stay there because God did not give us a spirit of fear (2 Timothy 1:7).

Walk in faith

It's one thing to say you have faith, and quite another to have your faith tested during challenging times. In Matthew 14:22-33, the disciples are not only afraid when they see Jesus walking on water, but Peter says, "Lord, if it be thou, bid me come unto thee on the water." (v 28). Amid the storms of life, we must walk in faith.

GRATEFUL

What are you grateful for today?

LISTENING

As you pray, ask God to help calm your fears about any challenges you are facing.

OBSERVATION

Read Mark 4:35–41.

WITNESS

Talk to someone about some aspect of your faith — either a time you did not believe or a time when you had to show great faith.

DAY 4–TIME FOR HOPE

Note to Self:

Good morning, Lord. So grateful to be alive. Your goodness and mercy are following me everywhere I go, and I thank you.

Going to church today. I am looking forward to focusing on you, Lord.

Full of hope,

DAY 4 — TIME FOR HOPE

"... Do not be afraid; only believe." (Mark 5:36)

God does not want us to feel hopeless or afraid. When we have hope in the Lord, our strength will not only be renewed, but we will not grow weary or faint. (Isaiah 40:31). In Mark 5, we find a parent faced with a seemingly hopeless situation. Instead of giving up hope, the father shows three things we must do when faced with challenges.

Timeout Takeaways

We must seek help from God

In Mark 5:22, Jarius, a ruler of the synagogue, fell at Jesus's feet, begging him to heal his daughter. "My daughter lie at the point of death: I pray thee, come and lay thy hands on her, that she may be healed; and she shall live." (v 23) Despite his position, Jarius was not too proud to ask for help.

We must humble ourselves before the Lord

That Jarius was a religious leader was interesting since many of the scribes and Pharisees were angry with Jesus for his teachings in the synagogues. It is likely that many of those people were friends with Jarius and would be disappointed he turned to Jesus for help. But Jarius needed a miracle. Like many of us when faced with a desperate situation, Jarius went to extreme lengths for his daughter.

We must stay focused

As Jesus and Jarius headed to see the girl, Jesus stopped to heal a woman with an issue of blood (v 25–34). After curing the woman, a friend tells Jarius that his daughter is dead and there is no need to bother Jesus anymore. When Jesus heard this, He told Jarius, "Be not afraid, only believe." (v 36) Do not give up hope.

GRATEFUL

What are you grateful for today?

LISTENING

As you pray, ask God to increase your faith and restore your hope over any challenge you are facing.

OBSERVATION

Read Mark 5:22.

WITNESS

Share your testimony about hope with someone.

DAY 5—TIME TO SUBMIT

Note to Self:

Good morning, Lord. It's Monday, and I am eager to start the week. I'm keen to continue looking for a job but I know I have a lot to do at work before I leave. Since I am at peace with my layoff, help me be a blessing to those around me. I submit to your will.

Totally committed,

DAY 5 — TIME TO SUBMIT

"Submit yourselves therefore to God. Resist the devil, and he will flee from you."

(James 4:7)

Submission can be hard. How often do we want to give up our plans for someone or something else? But a healthy, loving relationship with God involves submission. I must tell myself all the time, God knows what's best for me. I must go with His plan. But truth be told, I sometimes can't resist asking God, "Are you sure you want me to do this?" Just as Ananias did in Acts 9:10–19.

On his way to Damascus, Saul had an encounter with God that left him blind (v 3–9). In verse 10, we meet "a certain disciple at Damascus named Ananias." We know nothing about Ananias before this point except he is an ordinary man. The Scriptures do not describe him as a minister, or evangelist, or deacon, just a certain disciple who would answer God by saying, "Here I am, Lord." (v 10) The Lord Jesus tells Ananias to go to the house in Damascus where Saul is staying, "that he might receive his sight." (v 12) After hearing God's instructions, Ananias tells God about the evil Saul has done to believers of Jesus. But the Lord said, "Go thy way: for he is a chosen vessel unto me, to bear my name before the Gentiles, and kings, and the children of Israel." (v15) Ananias did as God asked. He laid his hands on Saul's eyes, and his sight was restored.

Timeout Takeaways

Answer when God calls

The Bible is full of examples of God speaking to people. When God called Jonah, not only did he ignore God, but he walked away from God. (Jonah 1:1–3) In contrast, when the Lord spoke to in a vision to Ananias, he said, "I am here, Lord?" This is the response God wants to hear from his children.

Be honest about how you feel

From what we know about Ananias, we see that he is a certain disciple (Acts 9:10) and a devout man (Acts 22:12). God not only knew Ananias, but He knew He could call him for this special assignment. So, when God asked him to go see Saul, he immediately let God know he had concerns, "Master, you can't be serious. Everybody's talking about this man and the terrible things he's been doing, his reign of terror against your people in Jerusalem!" (v 13) When we are honest with God about how we feel; He can speak directly to our concerns.

Submit to God's plans

Without another word of hesitation, Ananias goes off to see Saul. When he arrived at the house, he told Saul, "Brother Saul, the Master sent me, the same Jesus you saw on your way here. He sent me so you could see again and be filled with the Holy Spirit." (v 17) When Ananias laid hands on Saul, his eyesight was restored. Submission to God's plan results in blessings.

GRATEFUL

What are you grateful for today?

LISTENING

As you pray, ask God to help you identify any area of your life where you have not submitted entirely to His will.

OBSERVATION

Read Acts 9:10–19.

WITNESS

Talk to someone about your experience dealing with submission to God.

DAY 6—TIME TO LISTEN

Note to Self:

Thank you, God, for this day. I am so blessed. Thank you for my telephone interview. Not sure if the job in San Diego will be a good fit, but I appreciate the opportunity just to talk.

Unless you tell me differently, Lord, I am moving toward the job you are already working out for me. I am praying, Lord, that I listen to your Holy Spirit carefully. I don't want to miss what you have in store for me.

Forever grateful for your love,

DAY 6 — TIME TO LISTEN

"Making your ear attentive to wisdom and inclining your heart to understanding." (Proverbs 2:2)

We must position ourselves to hear God's voice. To learn more about how to listen, I went to 1 Samuel 3, where I discovered the story of Samuel and Eli.

At this point in Samuel's life, he is 12 years old and living with Eli. One night as Eli and Samuel where sleeping, Samuel heard a voice calling his name. As his sleeping quarters were very close to Eli's, who at this point in his life was weak and nearly blind, Samuel immediately ran to Eli, saying, "I am here." Eli told Samuel that he didn't call him and to go back to bed. Samuel heard his name again, and for a second time, he ran to Eli's bed. "I didn't call you. Go back to bed." When God called Samuel a third time, causing him to go to Eli a third time, Eli suddenly realized that it was God who was calling Samuel's name. Eli told Samuel what to say if the Lord called again. When the Lord called Samuel a fourth time, Samuel said, "Speak Lord. I am your servant, and I am listening." Once Samuel answered God, he received his assignment.

Timeout Takeaways

Expect a call anytime

Most of us like to take calls when we are free to talk. A message from God can come day or night. Even when the timing is not convenient for our schedules. The lesson I had to learn is that life doesn't always happen in the way I want.

God doesn't stop calling

Samuel had four chances to answer God. Just because we don't hear God or we want to ignore His voice, doesn't mean He will stop calling. In every situation, God has the perfect plan.

Be prepared to answer

When God calls Samuel a fourth time, he was ready to respond. Eventually, we must answer God's call. Once we learn how to recognize God's voice, we must answer with a willing heart.

GRATEFUL

What are you grateful for today?

LISTENING

As you pray, ask God to help you identify any area of your life where you have not submitted entirely to God's will.

OBSERVATION

Read 1 Samuel 2.

WITNESS

Talk to someone about your experience of hearing God's voice or ignoring God's voice.

DAY 7—TIME TO FORGIVE

Note to Self:

Thank you, God, for keeping me. It's been seven days since I got the news about my job. I can honestly say I am at peace. Some people I talked to at work thought I should be upset. But really, I'm not about to go down that road. If I hold on to anger, I'll just be playing right into the devil's hands.

But I know I need to protect my mind from negative thoughts. Help me, Lord, to walk with a loving and forgiving heart. I can't do it on my own.

Thankful heart,

> "Be kind to one another, tender-hearted, forgiving each other, just as God in Christ also has forgiven you." (Ephesians 4:32)

Sometimes it's hard to sit on the sidelines, especially if you are used to being in the game. When we are told to, 'sit this one out,' we sometimes let our emotions get the best of us as we look for reasons or people to blame. Before we know it, the enemy is right there, suggesting how we should feel about the situation and the people involved. Toxic thoughts lead us to believe our moment of timeout has been brought on by someone else. Our path down the road to unforgiveness set.

Whether someone else is to blame, we must take control of our thoughts and feelings. We cannot walk around with anger and unforgiveness in our heart. To avoid the pitfalls of unforgiveness, I examined the life of Joseph in Genesis chapters 37 to 45.

Timeout Takeaways

Joseph did not allow bitterness to control him

Despite being thrown in a hole and left for dead by his brothers, Joseph forgave them. How many times have you held onto unforgiveness because of what someone did to you? I'm sure we can all raise our hands. But unforgiveness not only causes bitterness, it also keeps us in bondage.

Joseph continues to show love

In spite of the hurt and pain he endured, Joseph invited his family to live in Goshen near him. I'm sure we can all relate to how hard it is sometimes to forgive our family members. But it can be done when we rely on God's Spirit to help us.

Joseph could see God's plan

Although Joseph endured evil, he continued to move forward per God's plan. "As for you, you meant evil against me, but God intended it for good; to bring it about that many people should be kept alive as they are today." (Genesis 50:20) Despite all that we go through, even during job layoffs, we must believe God is working it out for our good.

GRATEFUL

What are you grateful for today?

LISTENING

As you pray, ask God to help you identify anyone you need to forgive.

OBSERVATION

Read Genesis 45:9-15.

WITNESS

Talk to someone about how God led you to forgive someone.

WORDS OF ADVICE

I get angry every time I think about the day I was laid off.

For some people, a layoff can feel like a form of rejection. Holding on to those feelings to the point of anger is precisely what the devil wants us to do. God wants us to renew our mind (Rom. 12:2), change what we think about (Phil 4:8), and concentrate on Him (Isa 26:3).

Use a journal to write about how you feel, including:

- what makes you angry about being laid off?
- what makes you happy about leaving your job?
- what will you do every day when your job ends?
- what do you want your next job to be like?
- how will you ensure peace in your life during this time?

Make a prayer list using the information you write about in your journal. Ask God to help you:

- **heal** any hard feelings you have toward your former boss or employer
- **reveal** any sins you committed because of hurt feelings
- **deal** with the days and weeks ahead as you move forward

DAY 8 – TIME TO LOVE

Note to Self:

Good morning, Lord! Thank you for letting me see another great day!

Thank you for the most recent performance award that I just received at work! Yes, even on my way out the door you keep on blessing me. I am so grateful. This is the third time this year that I have been recognized for my work on one of my projects. Even amid the storm, your loving- kindness is better than life.

Show me how to love others the way you love me.

With much love,

> "A new commandment I give to you, that you love one another: just as I have loved you, you also are to love one another. By this, all people will know that you are my disciples if you have love for one another." (John 13:34–35)

Every follower of Jesus Christ is supposed to love. But when dealing with unpleasant people, have you ever asked yourself, "Surely, Jesus didn't mean to love everyone, did he?" It's a fair question. But every time I ask myself this question, I am reminded of John 13.

During his time on earth, Jesus showed love to many people. He healed the man with the withered hand (Matt 12:10). Jesus healed many who were sick with various diseases (Luke 4:40). He healed those who were deaf (Mark 7:37). To prepare for his departure, Jesus told the apostles to show love in the same way He had done during his ministry. Christ said people would recognize His disciples by the love they have for people (John 13:35). Jesus's new commandment was not optional. He expected the apostles to show love to everyone. He expects present-day believers to do the same.

Timeout Takeaways

Go the extra mile

In Matthew 9:18, a leader of the synagogue asks Jesus to come to his house to lay hands on his daughter who has died. Jesus got up from where he was and went with the man. To love people, we must sometimes go to them.

Go above and beyond

How far will you go to show your love for others? In Luke 5:17–39, we find a paralyzed man being carried by his friends to see Jesus. When the men could not get their friend through the front door, they lowered him through a hole in the roof (v 19). When Jesus saw how much faith they all had, he said, "Friend, your sins are forgiven" (v 20) and, "I tell you, stand up! Take your mat and go home." (v 24). The men showed love when they went above and beyond to get their friend to Jesus.

Go to great lengths

After the deaths of Saul and Jonathan in 1 Samuel 31, David asks, "Is there still anyone who is left of the house of Saul, that I may show him kindness for Jonathan's sake?" (2 Samuel 9:1) David wanted to show love to any remaining member of Saul's family, despite Saul making himself an enemy of the king before his death. David discovers that Jonathan's son, Mephibosheth is alive and living in the home of Machir the son of Ammiel, from Lo Debar. He instructs his servant to go to Lo Debar and bring Mephibosheth to his house where he can live and eat at the table of the king.

GRATEFUL

What are you grateful for today?

LISTENING

As you pray, ask God to help you show love toward others.

OBSERVATION

Read John 13:34–35.

WITNESS

Talk to someone about a time when God used people or a person to show you love.

DAY 9–TIME TO FOCUS

Note to Self:

Thank you, God, for my husband. He came up with a great idea: Let's go to the beach this weekend!

He didn't have to ask me twice. I will use my time at the beach to listen to you, God, and focus on any new opportunities you have for me.

Looking to the hills,

DAY 9 — TIME TO FOCUS

"Let your eyes look directly forward, and your gaze be straight before you."
(Proverbs 4:25)

There's no time for daydreaming during a timeout. It's easy for the mind to wander. When God calls a timeout in our lives, we must focus.

In Philippians 4:8–9, Paul offers the Philippian church advice on what they should and should not focus their attention on. Here's what I got out of this Scripture.

Timeout Takeaways

Concentrate on good thoughts

Realizing how easy it is to have negative thoughts, Paul reminds us all to not focus on things that are ugly or will cause us to become angry. How many times have we all relived an argument with a coworker in our mind? Or thoughts of being done wrong by our boss? Summing it all up, we must fill our minds and meditate on things true, noble, reputable, authentic, compelling, and gracious.

Don't let your mind run wild

The enemy wants to control our minds, especially during quiet times when we are waiting for direction from God. The more Satan can control our thoughts so we think about failures and fears, the better chance he has to make us sad and fearful.

Walk in peace

Finally, Paul tells the Philippians if they think about good things, the peace of God will walk with them (v 9). It's important to invite peace, Jehovah Shalom, into our lives daily. Jesus's desire is, "that in me you may have peace. In the world, you will have tribulation. But take heart; I have overcome the world." (John 16:33).

GRATEFUL

What are you grateful for today?

LISTENING

As you pray, ask God to help you stay focused.

OBSERVATION

Read Philippians 4:8–9.

WITNESS

Talk to someone about the benefits of staying positive or a time when you needed God to help adjust your focus.

DAY 10–TIME TO STUDY

Note to Self:

Thank you, God, for being a provider. Not only did you bring us safely to the beach for the weekend, but I cashed in my hotel reward points to pay for our room. Booyah!

Now it's time to study! Reading my Bible, listening to sermons, lots of prayers and alone time with God. Also, I found some interesting articles on how to start a business. Food for thought. ☺

Still looking to the hills,

DAY 10 — TIME TO STUDY

"Acquire wisdom! Acquire understanding! Do not forget nor turn away from the words of my mouth." (Proverbs 4:5)

One of the best times to study is during a timeout. As a lifelong learner, I quickly saw my time away from work as a chance to research ideas, explore new career options, and talk to people. But first I looked at Timothy to learn more about the benefits of studying.

In 2 Timothy 2, Paul relies on metaphors to describe how Timothy should approach Christian ministry. Each metaphor embodies the characteristics Timothy should show in his life as a minister. In verse 15, "Study to shew thyself approved unto God, a workman that needeth not to be ashamed, rightly dividing the word of truth," Paul encourages Timothy to seek God's approval and to study so he can handle and teach God's Word.

Another example on how to study can be found in Luke 10:38–39 where Jesus stops at the house of Martha and Mary. As Martha works, Mary, "sat at the Lord's feet and listened to his teaching." (v 39) Angry that her sister was not helping her, Martha asked Jesus to make Mary help her. But Jesus told Martha, "Mary has chosen the good part, which will not be taken away from her." (v 42)

Timeout Takeaways

Study to know

Paul encouraged Timothy to study to know God's Word — what it said. Paul knew it would not be acceptable for Timothy to know just a few Bible verses to impress people. As a pastor, he would need to know God's Word in such a way he could lead people to Christ.

Study to grow

For Mary to sit at the feet of Jesus showed her devotion to Him and the love she had for hearing Him teach. Rather than working all the time, Mary took the time to listen to Jesus, which helped her grow as a follower of Christ.

Study to flow

Both Timothy and Mary saw the benefit of having an in-depth knowledge of Christ. Every Christian must learn and know the truth of God's Word. Not that every Christian must be a Bible scholar. Studying God's Word will go a long way in helping to impact the lives of others.

GRATEFUL

What are you grateful for today?

LISTENING

As you pray, ask God to open your mind to learning something new.

OBSERVATION

Read 2 Timothy 2:15.

WITNESS

Talk to someone about your experience studying God's Word.

Note to Self:

Thank you, God, for life, health, and strength. I'm waking up with new revelations!

I can see now how easy it is to lose sight of the things that matter. Not the things that matter to man but the things that matter to you, Lord. Before I learned about my job layoff, my day started at 4 a.m. and did not end until 10 p.m. I moved from one thing to the next. From telephone calls to meetings to errands to homework to preparing dinner, I did whatever it took to get through the day. But I had lost sight of what mattered. I plan to use this time to cast off a few things.

New dawn. New day.

Casting my cares

DAY 11 — TIME TO CASTOFF

"For we walk by faith, not by sight." (2 Corinthians 5:7)

The Bible is full of examples where people's lives are changed in an instance. In Mark 10:49–51 we find Bartimaeus, a blind man, sitting by the roadside near Jericho. Hearing loud noises coming from the crowd, the man learns that Jesus is coming in his direction. Desperate, he shouts, "Jesus, Son of David, have mercy on me!" Despite being told to keep quiet by the local dignitaries, Bartimaeus cries louder, "Jesus, Son of David, have mercy on me!"

When Jesus tells the man to come to him, the man casts off his garment immediately and goes to Jesus. In an instant, Jesus restores the man's sight.

The restoration of Bartimaeus's sight is inspiring and left me asking, "What do you want me to see, Lord?" But the part of the story that touched me relates to the garment.

The garment that Bartimaeus threw aside was described as a cloak or a loose-fitting garment that someone likely gave him. But the clothing also represented what every disciple must do to follow Jesus — throw off the past. Here's what else I learned.

Timeout Takeaways

Speak up

Bartimaeus did not hesitate to ask Jesus for help. Don't bother telling everyone about your problems. Go to God in prayer immediately. Allow Him to speak to your heart.

Move quickly

When Jesus told Bartimaeus to come to him, he moved quickly. Don't waste time. When God calls, we must learn to run to Him immediately.

Let go

As Bartimaeus sprang to his feet and threw off his garment, he showed that he was eager to let go of his past. How many times have you tried to hold on to things and people you should have let go long ago? I'm guilty.

But not anymore. We must learn to let go and prepare for the great things God has planned for us.

GRATEFUL

What are you grateful for today?

LISTENING

As you pray, ask God to help you identify any negative things, or people, you need to remove from your life.

OBSERVATION

Read Mark 10:49–51

WITNESS

Talk to someone about a time when you had to move closer to God.

DAY 12–TIME TO OBEY

Note to Self:

Thanks for a beautiful weekend, Lord. You showed me so much. I'm going home today refreshed, renewed and prepared to obey your voice.

Claiming victory,

DAY 12 — TIME TO OBEY

"But be doers of the word, and not hearers only, deceiving yourselves."

(James 1:22)

How hard is it to listen to God? Especially when you think you have it all figured out? This is the story of my life, where I'm continually telling God, "I don't need your help. I've got it all worked out." To avoid making that mistake again, I turned my attention to 2 Kings 4.

In 2 Kings 4, we find a widow in trouble. The single mother told the prophet, Elisha, that she had to either pay her deceased husband's debt or surrender her sons as slaves. Elisha told the widow to fill as many vessels as possible with oil. Following Elisha's instructions carefully, the widow collected jugs and bowls, closed the door behind her, and started pouring. Before long, the widow and her sons had gathered as many vessels as they could find. When she gave Elisha a progress report, he told her to, "Go, sell the oil and pay your debts. You and your sons can live on what is left." (2 Kings 4:7)

The story opened my eyes to the power of being obedient to godly advice. This example of God's greatness shows that every believer must be prepared to obey and surrender to God's will. The story of the widow reminds me that God not only supplies all, but He has the perfect plan for my life.

Timeout Takeaways

Be obedient

When faced with problems in the past, related to jobs, money or family, I always thought my plan or approach was the best. I had to learn to go to God first and then listen to His instructions. In my mind, my plan always seemed right, but God's plan was still better.

Be open

In verses 3 and 4, Elisha gives the woman specific instructions on how to fill all the bowls and jugs she can find with oil. Elisha's orders included borrowing bowls from neighbors, going home and locking the door and filling each pitcher before setting them aside. Like the woman did not question Elisha's instructions, I had to learn to open my heart and follow God's instructions.

Be ready for overflow

The woman filled every jug she could find. It wasn't until she couldn't find any more pitchers that the oil stopped flowing. By obeying God's command, the woman made more than enough money to pay off her husband's debt. She experienced an overflow from God.

GRATEFUL

What are you grateful for today?

LISTENING

As you pray, ask God to help you become more obedient day by day.

OBSERVATION

Read 2 Kings 4:7.

WITNESS

Talk to someone about a time when you obeyed God's voice.

Note to Self:

Good morning, Lord. Waking up grateful today. Also, I am very thankful for all the people I have met throughout my career.

I also thank you for my call with Judy, one of the executives at work. * She wanted to check on me, which was nice. Although she does not have a job to offer me, she told me she would let me know if a job became available. I told her thanks but asked her to consider my coworker, Cindy,* who is also getting laid off. Cindy loves the company and doesn't want to leave. I pray that she will stay.

I know people might think it's crazy, Lord, to think about someone else having a job knowing I soon won't have one. But I know you asked me to tell Judy to consider Cindy for a reason. Show me what you want me to do and where you want me to go.

In Your Service,

*Not the person's real name.

DAY 13 -- TIME TO SACRIFICE

"Do not neglect to do good and to share what you have, for such sacrifices are pleasing to God." (Hebrews 13:16)

When was the last time you made a sacrifice? For a family member, a friend or even a stranger? To sacrifice means to give up something, which isn't always easy. But God offers us a different perspective in the book of Esther.

Mordecai, Esther's cousin, told her about the order to have all Jews killed. He begged her to go to the king, her husband, to have the order reversed. Esther knew anyone who went to see the king without being called first could be killed. Before her meeting with the king, she called for and took part in a three-day fast for the Jewish people. After the fast, Esther told the king about Haman's plot against the Jewish people. The Jewish people were saved, and they hung Haman on the same gallows he had prepared for Mordecai.

Timeout Takeaways

Everything happens for a reason

Nothing happens by chance or coincidence. God's timing is providential. I came to realize that if I was selected as one of the many employees being laid off; it was all a part of God's plan for my life.

Practice humility

Although Esther was the queen, she did not demand that the king see her or that her people be saved from destruction. Instead, she was humble in her approach.

Don't be afraid to stand up for others

Esther knew they could kill her for asking to see the king during a time when her presence was not requested. But she courageously said, "If I perish, I perish." (4:16).

GRATEFUL

What are you grateful for today?

LISTENING

As you pray, ask God to help you deal with making sacrifices.

OBSERVATION

Read Esther 4:16.

WITNESS

Talk to someone about a time when you had to make a sacrifice.

DAY 14 — TIME FOR PATIENCE

Note to Self:

Good morning, Lord. Thank you for waking me up to start a new day made by you.

As of today, I have sent out over 50 resumes. So, I'm just waiting to see if I get a nibble from one of these companies. As you know, waiting is not my strong suit. But I like how you have worked with me over the years to get those feelings in check. ☺

Help me, Lord, to understand waiting according to your plan for my life. Still grateful and excited about the day ahead.

Patiently waiting.

DAY 14 — TIME FOR PATIENCE

"Rejoice in hope, be patient in tribulation, be constant in prayer."

(Romans 12:12)

Waiting is hard. We live in a world that offers instant gratification, attention, and information. Even with all the promises that God provides, waiting can be a challenge.

In Genesis 15, "the word of the LORD came to Abram in a vision, saying, 'Do not be afraid, Abram. I am your shield, your exceedingly great reward.'" In a moment of honesty, Abraham let God know that while he appreciated the promise, it still concerned him that he didn't have any children. God reminded Abraham of the promises made to him in Genesis 12:2 and 13:15–16, where He told Abraham He would have heirs as numerous as the stars.

But when God did not fulfill the promise as quickly as Abraham and Sarah wanted, Sarah suggested that Abraham have a baby with Hagar, Sarah's handmaid (Genesis 16). After Hagar gave birth to Ishmael when Abraham was 100 and Sarah was 99, God's promise was fulfilled through the birth of Isaac (Genesis 17:15).

Sarah and Abraham did not wait patiently for the promise of God. Instead, they took matters into their own hands and went against the will of God. This is what I learned from their experience.

Timeout Takeaways

God is a promise keeper

God knows how to keep a promise. God promised Abraham in Genesis 12:2 and 13:15–16 that he would give him an heir. God's ability to make and keep promises is clear throughout the Bible. In a conversation with Jeremiah, God said, "and I always rise early to keep a promise." (Jeremiah 1:12)

Move in God's time

I can remember a time when I was just like Abraham and Sarah. If God didn't move fast enough, I took care of it for Him. But I had to learn to wait. Yes, God hastens to perform His word (Jeremiah 1:12) but in His time, "Don't let it escape your notice, dear friends, that with the Lord a single day is like a thousand years and a thousand years are like a single day." (2 Peter 3:8)

The baby will come

Although God makes a promise to Abraham about having a baby in Genesis 12, it is not until Genesis 17 when the baby, Isaac, arrives. A 14-year gap. But as Paul reminds us in Galatians 4:23, Ishmael was born according to the flesh, and Isaac but was born as the result of a divine promise. God can give us everything we ask for in the blink of an eye. But sometimes, He makes us wait. Waiting allows us to exercise our spiritual muscles in patience, trust, and surrender.

GRATEFUL

What are you grateful for today?

LISTENING

As you pray, ask God to help you deal with patience.

OBSERVATION

Read Romans 12:12.

WITNESS

Talk to someone about a time when you had to wait and how God delivered.

WORDS OF ADVICE

I'm so used to being busy that I don't know how to slow down.

In our fast-paced world, it can be hard to slow down. But Jesus did it (Matt 14:23), and every believer who wants a closer walk with God must do it too. The spiritual discipline of silence is the voluntary and temporary break from talking, while the discipline of solitude involves privacy with God.

Below are tips on how to include silence and solitude in your timeout period and beyond.

- Spend 10, 30 or 60 seconds consciously focused on Christ. In these few seconds, and without talking, thank God for His grace and mercy.

- Schedule time in your calendar to sit quietly with God. Take your Bible to a quiet room. Ask God to speak to you through His word. If necessary, ask your family not to disturb you for the next 10, 30 or 60 minutes.

Plan a time when you can get away either for a morning or afternoon retreat or for a few days. Before you go, create a plan outlining how you would like to spend your time away with God.

DAY 15—TIME FOR SURRENDER

Note to Self:

Thank you for this day, Lord Jesus. I am grateful today for all that you continue to do for me.

Part of me cannot believe I am getting laid off, at age 51, for the third time in my career. I naively thought I would retire at this company. But I see now that is not part of your plan, so I surrender, God.

Have your way in my life. Take me where you want me to go.

Trusting you,

DAY 15 — TIME TO SURRENDER

"Submit yourselves therefore to God. Resist the devil, and he will flee from you." (James 4:7)

Giving in to God's plan can be hard. Especially when you think you have the perfect plan all worked out. I have been there so many times. To avoid going down that road again, I studied the book of Jonah.

In chapter one of the book of Jonah, God told Jonah to speak to the people in Nineveh. Instead of submitting to God's will, Jonah runs in the opposite direction to Tarshish. How many of us can relate to how Jonah must have felt? God calls, and we pretend not to hear His voice. But God doesn't give up so quickly. He slows Jonah down by having him swallowed by a giant sea creature. Jonah finally tells God he will preach to the people of Nineveh. The story of Jonah showed me three things not to do in learning how to surrender to God's will.

Timeout Takeaways

Don't run from God

It seems like an easy decision to not run from God. Surely Jonah knew God would find him. But many of us, myself included, have tried to run from God. But just like God continued to pursue Jonah, He will not give up or stop calling us either. Eventually, we must stop running.

Don't take down others

Jonah quickly finds a ship going to Tarshish. Once the boat is at sea, God sends a storm. The people on the ship soon learned that Jonah caused the storm. Jonah admits the truth and tells the men if they throw him overboard, they will live.

Don't question God's mercy

When God calls us with specific instructions, we should take ownership of God's actions. In chapter four, we learn that Jonah is mad at God for not destroying Nineveh. Despite delivering God's message to the people of Nineveh, Jonah is angry because God does not destroy the people. God can extend His mercy to who He wants when He wants.

GRATEFUL

What are you grateful for today?

LISTENING

As you pray, ask God to help you deal with surrender.

OBSERVATION

Read Jonah 1:1–3.

WITNESS

Talk to someone about a time when you ran when you heard God's voice.

DAY 16—TIME TO WRESTLE

Note to Self:

Good morning, Lord. Waking up grateful to see another day.

In about 15 days, I will be officially out of a job. Looking forward to the future but God, I want answers to my questions. 'What do you want me to do next?' 'Where do you want me to work next?' 'Why is this happening now 45 days before the end of the year?'

I'm wrestling with so many thoughts in my brain. Help me, Lord.

Looking for answers,

DAY 16—TIME TO WRESTLE

"And Jacob was left alone. And a man wrestled with him until the breaking of the day." (Genesis 32:24)

In Genesis 32, Jacob is preparing to meet his brother, Esau, and his 400-man army. Fearful, Jacob divides his tribe of wives and children into two camps just in case Esau plans to destroy him. Before seeing Esau, Jacob spends the night alone praying when he encounters a man who wrestles with him all night. At some point, Jacob realizes the man is God. God dislocates Jacob's hip, but Jacob refuses to let God go, saying, "I will not let you go unless you bless me." (Genesis 32:26). God blesses Jacob, who he renames Israel. Despite feeling weak and walking with a limp, Jacob's faith is strong as he moves forward to meet Esau.

Timeout Takeaways

New faith

Before Jacob wrestled with God, he was fearful of meeting his estranged brother Esau. After the encounter, his faith was renewed. Despite our struggles in life If we put our faith in God, we will win.

New determination

Despite wrestling with God all night, Jacob would not go until he received a blessing. Instead of allowing the enemy to lure us away from God, sometimes we must stay in God's presence to receive a blessing.

New identity

God blessed Jacob with a new identity. Gone was his former identity as one who deceived. Going forward, Jacob was known as Israel. As I prepared to say goodbye to my job, I asked God to bless me to walk into the new identity he was making for me.

GRATEFUL

What are you grateful for today?

LISTENING

As you pray, ask God to help you deal with any troubling issues in your life.

OBSERVATION

Read.

WITNESS

Talk to someone about a time when God brought you through a troubling time in your life.

DAY 17—TIME TO SPEAK

Note to Self:

Good morning, Lord. Grateful for another day and everything you are doing in my life.

After sending out emails to let my coworkers know I would leave and how to access the work I have been doing on their projects, I received a lot of emails and phone calls of support. While I have responded to each email, I haven't talked to everyone yet. Some people want to meet with me while others want to talk over the phone. When I do, Lord, please give me the words to say. Layoffs can be stressful for many people at work, not just me or the others getting laid off. Guard my tongue. Let your Spirit speak through me. Let the words of my mouth be acceptable.

DAY 17 — TIME TO SPEAK

"Set a guard, O Lord, over my mouth; keep watch over the door of my lips!" (Psalm 141:3)

It's important to pay attention to what we say. Words can lift or tear down. In the days leading up to my layoff at work, I was cautious not to say anything negative about my boss, my department or the company I was leaving. I knew a journey down that road would only leave me bitter, and all alone. Instead, I spoke the words of David in Psalm 141:3, "Set a guard, O Lord, over my mouth, keep watch over the door of my lips!" My prayers were answered.

If we invite God into our conversation, he will come to the rescue. When Jeremiah tells God that he doesn't know what to say because he is too young to be his messenger, God says, "Do not say, 'I am only a youth'; for to all to whom I send you, you shall go, and whatever I command you, you shall speak." (v 7) God calms Jeremiah's fears by touching his mouth to give him the words to say. If we let him, God will direct our speech.

Timeout Takeaways

Lock your lips

David asked God to put a guard over his mouth to prevent him from saying anything he would regret. As some of my coworkers approached me to talk about all the layoffs going on in the company, it was clear they expected me to be hurt or angry. But I resisted the urge to say anything negative.

Freeze your fingers

David's cry to God reflected his fear of sin. He did not want to give in to the temptation of using sinful words. Like David, my prayer was for God to help me use the most appropriate words even through email and social media networks. I allowed God to help me walk in Colossians 4:6.

Sanctify your speech

When David wrote Psalm 141, Saul was chasing him. But even in such a stressful situation, David knew he could not control his tongue by his strength. So, he prayed to God for help. In the days leading up to my final day at work, I allowed God to take control of my speech, being very intentional about my choice of words.

GRATEFUL

What are you grateful for today?

LISTENING

As you pray, ask God to help you find the words for every conversation.

OBSERVATION

Read Psalm 141:1–4.

WITNESS

Talk to someone about a time when the Spirit of God helped you stay quiet.

DAY 18—TIME TO FELLOWSHIP

Note to Self:

Good morning, Lord. Thank you for today's wake-up call.

Grateful for all the doors you are opening. I appreciate all the calls and emails from recruiters. I am meeting many people on my journey. I see every interaction as an opportunity to get closer to what you have planned for me.

Looking forward to going to church tomorrow. I know Satan wants me to stay home, away from people, but I know where your Spirit is, there is liberty.

Free to worship.

DAY 18 — TIME TO FELLOWSHIP

"Not neglecting to meet together, as is the habit of some, but encouraging one another, and all the more as you see the Day drawing near."
(Hebrews 10:25)

When the cares of life weigh us down, we sometimes want to withdraw from our friends and family. Having gone down that road before during my first job layoff in 1995, I knew I did not want to repeat the same mistake. I went to the book of Acts to learn more about fellowship.

The Greek word for fellowship is *koinonia*, which means to share in something. In Acts 2, fellowship was one of the integral parts of the early church, "And they continued steadfastly in the apostles' doctrine and fellowship, in the breaking of bread, and in prayers." (v 42). Making fellowship a priority, members of the early church established relationships, partnerships, companionship, and stewardship. Individually and collectively, they took part in every fellowship opportunity.

Timeout Takeaways

Sharing our struggles

Life is tough. Acts 2:42 illustrates how the Christian life includes fellowship. To avoid isolation, I looked for opportunities to fellowship with other brothers and sisters in Christ. I went to Bible study, Sunday school, and women's fellowship events.

Sharing our faith

People in the early church relied on the apostles to teach them about Christ (v 42). Today, regular church attendance is essential. Yes, there are dozens of Christian television shows that air on Sundays. But the Bible tells us we are to gather. (Hebrews 10:25).

Sharing our victories

There was evidence of God's power through many signs and wonders (v 43). It's good to know how God is blessing people around us. The chance to meet with other believers means sharing and hearing stories about God's grace.

GRATEFUL

What are you grateful for today?

LISTENING

As you pray, ask God to help you stay connected to friends and family.

OBSERVATION

Read Acts 2:42-47

WITNESS

Talk to someone about a time when fellowship helped you get through a tough time.

DAY 19—TIME TO GIVE

Note to Self:

Lord Jesus, you are so good. Not just for what you have done but for who you are as the King of Kings. All that I have needed, your hand has provided, Lord. Thank you.

During my upcoming timeout, I plan to help other people pursuing the plans you have given to them. Because you have blessed me so much, I am going to offer my help and knowledge to others freely.

DAY 19-TIME TO GIVE

"Give, and it will be given to you. Good measure, pressed down, shaken together, running over, will be put into your lap. For with the measure you use it will be measured back to you." (Luke 6:38)

The Bible tells us that God loves a cheerful giver (2 Corinthians 9:7). I am a firm believer that to be cheerful about giving; learn from the Master. My lessons on giving started when I was 18 years old when I attended Sunday school and learned a lesson on tithing. Since then, God has shown me how to give in every season of my life. During my layoff in 2001, I was intentional about giving. Besides serving at church and in my community, I also tithed from every source of income that came my way.

David knew how to honor God. In 2 Samuel 24:18–25, Araunah offered to give David a threshing floor at no charge, "Let my lord the king take and offer up whatever seems good to him." (v 22) But David did not want to give God something that cost him nothing. "No. I've got to buy it from you for a good price; I'm not going to offer God, my God, sacrifices that are no sacrifice." I appreciate David's attitude on giving to God. He embraces the generosity described in Ecclesiastes 11:6, "In the morning sow your seed, and in the evening, withhold not your hands, for you know not which shall prosper, whether this or that, or whether both alike will be good."

Timeout Takeaways

Willing to give

Araunah had great respect for David. When he saw David approaching his house, he ran outside and bowed before him. His heart was open and willing to give David anything he needed, including the threshing floor at whatever price David suggested.

Able to give

Araunah had a generous spirit. Although he had been a king of the Jebusites, Araunah did not offer the threshing floor to David out of obligation or threat. Instead, Araunah was humble in his offering to David.

Ready to give

Why did David refuse Araunah's offer? Because David did not want to give God something that cost him nothing. He came to Araunah prepared to provide him with money for the threshing floor. David was ready to sacrifice for God.

GRATEFUL

What are you grateful for today?

LISTENING

As you pray, ask God to help you deal with giving.

OBSERVATION

Read Ecclesiastes 11:6.

WITNESS

Talk to someone about a time when God asked you to give to a person in need.

DAY 20—TIME FOR BATTLE

Note to Self:

Good morning, Lord. Thank you for letting me see another day. Thank you for carrying me through the fight. I'm hearing a lot of complaining, doubt, fear, and negative comments in these last days at work. Oh, I know people mean well, but seriously folks: not helping at all.

Protect my mind, Lord, as I go into battle. Taking the sword of the Spirit which is your word, God.

DAY 20 — TIME FOR BATTLE

"For our battle is not against blood and flesh, but against the rulers, against the authorities, against the cosmic rulers of this darkness, against the spiritual forces of evil in the heavenly places." (Ephesians 6:12)

Life often feels like a battle. We go from fighting traffic to trying to beat the clock. We face challenges at work, at home and at church. Sometimes it feels like Satan uses anything and everyone to knock us down. "But thanks be to God, who gives us the victory through our Lord Jesus Christ." (1 Corinthians 15:57) Each time I go onto the battlefield, I turn to Ephesians 6:10–20 because it offers the information about spiritual warfare in the New Testament.

Paul begins this portion of the letter with the adjective, "finally," or "from now on," to signify his final desires before closing the letter. In verse 10, Paul encourages Ephesus to "be strong in the Lord," before instructing them to put on the whole armor of God in verse 11 to stand against the schemes of the devil. Paul explains the armor each believer should *have* (v 13-14) to be prepared (v 15) and the parts of the armor each believer must *take* (v 16-17) when faced with certain aspects of spiritual warfare. The remaining verses, 18–20, outline how prayer and perseverance will help believers combat spiritual forces.

Timeout Takeaways

Take a walk

In the same way, a soldier needs sturdy, protective shoes for battle, every believer must go into battle armed with the gospel (v 15). In being prepared, as Paul suggests, followers of Christ be flexible and ready to share the gospel.

Take a shield

Spiritual warfare is ongoing. The darts fired in ancient combat came in significant numbers from all sides. Satan will use the lies, guilt, fear, imaginations and more as fiery darts. Your shield, as a form of your faith, will combat any fiery darts that come your way.

Take a helmet

A soldier would not go into battle without a helmet. The helmet of salvation that Paul describes protects us from discouragement. During your battle, Satan will try to discourage you in such a way that you will give up or retreat. Don't let him win.

GRATEFUL

What are you grateful for today?

LISTENING

As you pray, ask God to help you deal with any struggles in your life.

OBSERVATION

Read Ephesians 6:10–20.

WITNESS

Talk to someone about a time God protected you.

DAY 21—TIME TO WIN

Note to Self:

Good morning, Lord! Waking up with a grateful heart today.

Tomorrow is Thanksgiving, but I have been full of thanksgiving for the past 21 days! I'm so grateful for all the love and grace you have shown me. As of today, I have sent out nearly 100 resumes, had one telephone interview, several calls from recruiters and interviews set for December. Thanks for opening doors. Please lead me to the next chapter in my career.

Next week is my last week of work. Lead me in giving my coworkers all the files and materials they need to move forward. As I prepare to leave, I wish the company and my coworkers all the best. I read this in the Message Bible:

> *In the Messiah, in Christ, God leads us from place to place in one perpetual victory parade. Through us, he brings knowledge of Christ. Everywhere we go, people breathe in the exquisite fragrance. (2 Corinthians 2:14)*

Looking forward to the future.

Victorious.

DAY 21 — TIME TO WIN

"But thanks be to God, who gives us the victory through our Lord Jesus Christ." (1 Corinthians 15:57)

Everyone wants to win. Whether we compete against opponents or we enter a race towards our personal goals, we believe our determination will lead us to victory.

A great example of a believer with a winning attitude is the Canaanite woman in Matthew 15:21–28. In her appeal to Jesus, the woman begged Jesus to heal her daughter. She never gave up hope He would help her. Instead, she showed her faith. In doing so, the Bible states that Jesus gave in. "Oh woman, your faith is something else. What you want is what you get! Right then her daughter became well." (Matthew 15:28)

As I deal with life's challenges, including my job layoff, I know I need to activate my faith and stand on the promises of God.

Timeout Takeaways

Don't give up

Jesus did not respond to the woman immediately. As she continued to chase Jesus, the apostles urged Jesus to send her away. But the woman did not give up.

Don't lose faith

The Canaanite woman knew who Jesus was, "Have mercy on me, O Lord, thou Son of David" (v 22). She had faith in the healing power of Jesus Christ.

Don't be afraid

Despite being a Canaanite, or a Gentile, the woman was not afraid to ask Jesus to heal her daughter. Since her daughter was demon-possessed, the woman interceded on behalf of her daughter.

GRATEFUL

What are you grateful for today?

LISTENING

As you pray, ask God to help you be victorious once your timeout is over.

OBSERVATION

Read Matthew 15:21–28

WITNESS

Talk to someone about a time when you overcame an obstacle.

WORDS OF ADVICE

I'm ashamed to let people know that I am not working right now.

Part of Satan's plan to keep us feeling ashamed and fearful is to isolate us. He wants us to believe that not having a job or being appointed to lead the team is something to be ashamed of. Don't let him trick you. Second Timothy 1:7 reminds us that, "God gave us a spirit not of fear but of power and love and self-control."

In preparation for sharing your news with others, try the following tips.

- Write a brief elevator speech explaining why you are not working.

- Stick with the facts. Don't add speculation or display anger.

- Don't add any negative comments to your speech. Doing so will only make you look bad.

- Let people know what you plan to focus on until you find a new job. For example, volunteer work in the community or taking care of a family member.

While this book only highlights 21 days, my story continues. The Spirit of God gave me additional topics to study well into the following year. It wasn't long before I realized that God's plan for my timeout period was to abide on Him (John 15:7).

As for the next phase of my career, I continue to ask God to lead me. Since leaving my corporate position, I have been blessed to study, research new ideas, work on assignments that help other people reach their goals and serve God's people through my local church. Also, God has blessed me to live life on my terms through my new business and to publish my first book. The best part of all has been spending more time with my husband and son, including traveling to new places and seeing new things.

One of the biggest lessons learned has been the power of a renewed mind. There is a constant battle between the flesh and the Spirit. On my own, I knew I would lose this fight, so I turned to the truth and decided to:

- Set my mind on the things of the Spirit (Romans 8:5-6)

- Trust the Lord with all my heart (Proverbs 3:5)

- Choose my words carefully (Ephesians 4:29)

Was it easy? Not always. Was it necessary? Absolutely! My struggles between the flesh and the Spirit have gone on long enough. By following God's Word, I can walk securely and sleep without worry (Proverbs 3:23-24). Praise the Lord!

ACKNOWLEDGMENTS

This book would not be possible without the help of many wonderful, loving people. I'm grateful for all the support I've received from family, friends, and mentors. I am grateful to God for blessing me continuously and for being the lifter of my head. I'm grateful for my husband, Kelvin, for always encouraging me and for being my best friend for life. I'm grateful for my son, Cole, who loves to laugh and inspire me with great stories. I'm grateful for my mother, Edna Brown, and my aunt, Jeffie Jackson, for always allowing me to be creative. I'm grateful for my brother, James Brown, for pushing me to go far and sometimes joining me on the journey. I'm grateful to my in-laws, Pam and Karsten, for being a loving sister and brother, and to my late mother-in-law, Beverly Tyson, for her love and support. I'm grateful for my spiritual parents, Pastor T.L. and Elder Rebecca Carmichael for walking me through God's Word and always encouraging me to soar. I'm grateful to Robin Byrd and Lucy Levett for always listening to my bright ideas and for encouraging me to go for it. Finally, I'm grateful to the many people I haven't explicitly mentioned who pray for and encourage me, thank you.

ABOUT THE AUTHOR

Karen Brown Tyson has a Master of Arts degree in Christian Ministry and postgraduate certificates in Christian Leadership, Theological Studies and Biblical Studies from Liberty University Rawlings School of Divinity. Her ministry concentration focuses on the expository teaching of the Word of God in the areas of spiritual discipline, discipleship, leadership, apologetics and New Testament theology.

Karen has served in God's kingdom in a variety of ways including her most recent assignments with the Deacon's Wives, Women, Youth, Evangelism, Navigational and Helps ministries at her church, Elevation Baptist Church. Karen also serves as the Dean of the Elevation Bible Institute where she teaches courses on spiritual discipline, evangelism, and Christian apologetics.

Karen is a graduate of the Jerry Jenkins Christian Writer's Guild apprentice program. As a writer, she has developed several Christian ministry tools and training materials for her local church. Some of her work includes: *Understanding Your Spiritual Gifts; As We Worship: A Guide for Deacons' Wives*; and *Something to Talk About: A Speaker's Guide.*

Karen and her husband of 23 years, Kelvin, have one son and they live in North Carolina.

NOTES

Day 1

Boice, James Montgomery *Psalm, An Expositional Commentary, Volumes 1* (Grand Rapids, Michigan: Baker Books, 1994)

Day 2

Guzik, David. "Study Guide for 2 Kings 20." Blue Letter Bible. 7 Jul, 2006. Web. 9 Jul, 2018.

Day 8

Guzik, David. "Study Guide for Luke 5 and 2 Samuel 9." Blue Letter Bible. 21 Feb, 2017.

Day 10

Jamieson, Robert; Fausset, A. R.; Brown, David. Jamieson, Fausset, and Brown's Commentary on the Whole Bible.

Köstenberger, Andreas J.; Kellum, L. Scott; Quarles, Charles L. The Cradle, the Cross, and the Crown (Kindle Locations 18077-18081). B&H Publishing Group. Kindle Edition.

Day 11

Guzik, David. "Study Guide for Mark 10." Blue Letter Bible. 21 Feb, 2017.

Day 13

Whitney, Donald S. Spiritual Disciplines for the Christian Life with Bonus Content (Pilgrimage Growth Guide) (p. 185). NavPress. Kindle Edition.

Day 14

Genesis 15, 16, and 17 (KJV) - After these things the word." Blue Letter Bible.

Day 15

Jamieson, Robert; Fausset, A. R.; Brown, David. Jamieson, Fausset, and Brown's Commentary on the Whole Bible.

Day 16

Guzik, David. "Study Guide for Genesis 32." Blue Letter Bible. 21 Feb, 2017.

Day 17

Henry, Matthew. "Commentary on Psalms 141." Blue Letter Bible. 1 Mar, 1996.

Day 18

Guzik, David. "Study Guide for Acts 2." Blue Letter Bible. 21 Feb, 2017.

Day 19

Guzik, David. "Study Guide for 2 Samuel 24." Blue Letter Bible. 21 Feb, 2017.

Henry, Matthew. "Commentary on 2 Samuel 24." Blue Letter Bible. 1 Mar, 1996.

Day 20

Guzik, David. "Study Guide for Ephesians 6." Blue Letter Bible. 21 Feb, 2017.

Hoehner, Harold W. Ephesians: An Exegetical Commentary, 16160-16161.

MacDonald, Margaret Y. Sacra Pagina: Colossians and Ephesians. © 2000, © 2008 with updated bibliography by Order of Saint Benedict, Collegeville, Minnesota. All rights reserved.

Day 21

Guzik, David. "Study Guide for Matthew 15." Blue Letter Bible. 21 Feb, 2017.

INSPIRATION

What inspires you? Did you read anything that motivates you? Take note.

THANKS FOR READING, TIME TO REFRESH!

If you enjoyed this book, please consider sharing the message with others.

- Mention the book in a Twitter update, Facebook post, Pinterest pin, blog post, or upload a picture to Instagram.

- Recommend the book to people in your small group study, book club, workplace and classes.

- Pick up a copy for someone you know who would be inspired by the book.

- Share a book review on Amazon .

Visit my website at www.karenbrowntyson.com to learn more about my next book, Time to Reset.